Farm Machines

Milking Machines

Connor Dayton

PowerKiDS press™

New York

Published in 2012 by The Rosen Publishing Group, Inc.
29 East 21st Street, New York, NY 10010

First Edition

Editor: Jennifer Way
Designer: Greg Tucker

Photo Credits: Cover, p. 11 © www.iStockphoto.com/BanksPhotos; pp. 4–5, 7, 9, 13, 21, 23, 24 Shutterstock.com; p. 15 © www.iStockphoto.com/Tanuki Photography; pp. 16–17 S. Meltzer/PhotoLink/Getty Images; p. 19 Graeme Norways/Getty Images.

Library of Congress Cataloging-in-Publication Data

Dayton, Connor.
 Milking machines / [text by Connor Dayton]. — 1st ed.
    p. cm. — (Farm machines)
 Includes index.
 ISBN 978-1-4488-4945-1 (library binding) — ISBN 978-1-4488-5040-2 (pbk.) — ISBN 978-1-4488-5041-9 (6-pack)
 1. Milking machines—Juvenile literature. I. Title.
 SF247.D29 2012
 637'.1240284—dc22
                              2010050071

Manufactured in the United States of America

CPSIA Compliance Information: Batch #WS11PK: For Further Information contact Rosen Publishing, New York, New York at 1-800-237-9932

Contents

Milk comes from cows on **dairy farms**. Most American milk comes from California.

Cows must be milked twice each day.

Farmers milk the cows
using milking machines.

Many cows can be milked at once.

Milkers pump the milk from the cow.

First the farmer cleans the cow's teats. Then the farmer puts the milkers on them.

The milk from each cow is tested. This makes sure it is clean.

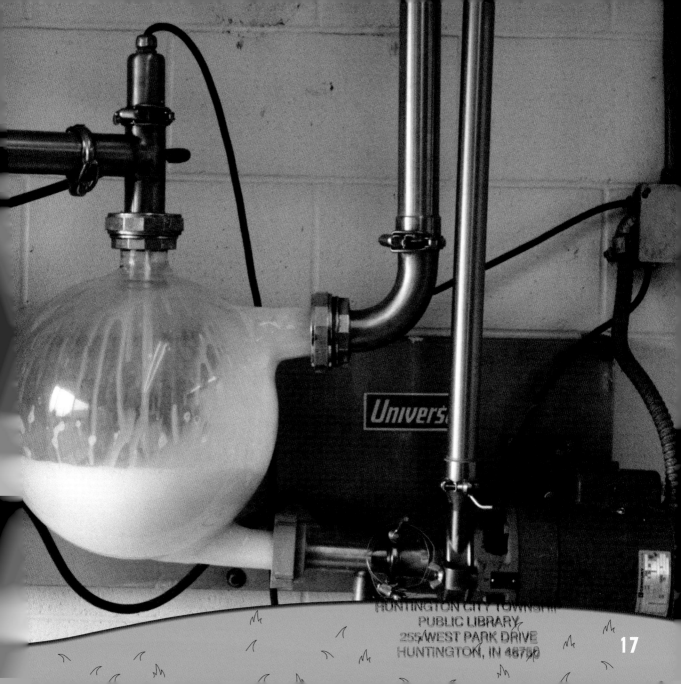

The milk goes through **tubes** into buckets. Then it goes into a **tank**.

The tank's job is to cool the milk.

Next the milk is packaged. It is then taken to stores and sold.

Words to Know

dairy farm

milkers

tank

tubes

Index

Web Sites

Due to the changing nature of Internet links, PowerKids Press has developed an online list of Web sites related to the subject of this book. This site is updated regularly. Please use this link to access the list:
www.powerkidslinks.com/farm/milking/